GOVERNMENT SERIES BOOK ONE

AMERICAN GOVERNMENT: HOW IT WORKS

Second Revised Edition

Dr. Marilyn Thypin
Lynne Glasner

Consultant:
Dr. Kenneth Job
Emeritus Professor
William Paterson College

Entry Publishing Inc.
New York

Acknowledgements
Cover design: Carol Gildar
Line art by Carol Gildar: pp. 21, 81
Second edition edited by David Follansbee
Imagesetting by Robert Schaffel

Photo credits:
Marilyn Thypin, pp. 1, 11, 12, 13, 79, 82, 85, 87
National Archives, p. 3
Architect of the Capitol, pp. 6, 19
R.D. Ward, Department of Defense, p. 8
Susan Biddle, The White House, pp. 17, 59
The White House, p. 24
Reuters/Bettman, p. 25
John F. Kennedy Library, p. 26
U.S. Department of Agriculture, p. 30
Michael Evans, The White House, p. 32
UPI, pp. 33, 53, 55, 57, 65
Office of Senator Claiborne Pell, p. 39
George OHL Withers, p. 41
Bob Black, p. 42
Ankers Capitol Photographers, p. 45
National Geographic Society, p. 48
Library of Congress, p. 50
J. Issac, The United Nations, p. 56
Office of Governor Ann Richards, p. 70
Black Star, p. 72

ISBN: 0-941342-19-0 (Book 1)
ISBN: 0-941342-23-9 (series)

Copyright © 1993, Entry Publishing, Inc.
All rights reserved. Published in 1993.
No part of this publication can be reproduced, stored in a retrieval system, or tansmitted in any form or by any means, electornic, mechanical or photocopying, recording, or otherwise, without the permission of the publisher.

Published by Entry Publishing Inc.
27 West 96th Street
New York, NY 10025

Printed in the United States of America
0 1 2 3 4 5 6 7 8 9

Table of Contents

CHAPTER 1
Government and the Law 1
    What is a government? 3
    Laws 4

CHAPTER 2
Levels of Government in the United States 6
    The federal government 8
    The state governments 9
    The local governments 10
    How the three levels of government work together 11

CHAPTER 3
The Three Branches of the Federal Government. 16
    The executive branch 17
    The legislative branch 18
    The judicial branch 19
    Checks and balances 20

CHAPTER 4
The Executive Branch of the Federal Government 24
    The President 25
    The Vice President 27
    The Cabinet 28
    The President and Congress 31

CHAPTER 5
The Legislative Branch of the Federal Government 34
    The Senate 35
    The House of Representatives 35
    How a bill becomes a law 37
    Congress and the American people 40

CHAPTER 6
The Judicial Branch of the Federal Government 45
    Cases in federal courts 46
    The Supreme Court 47

CHAPTER 7
The Legislative Branch and the Constitution 50
    How amendments become part of the Constitution 51
    The amendments to the Constitution 52
    Laws and the Supreme Court 54
    People's rights and the Supreme Court 56

CHAPTER 8
The United States As a World Power 59
    Kinds of government 60
    The United States and other countries 63
    The United Nations 66

CHAPTER 9
The State Governments 68
    How a state government works 69
    Ways to make state laws 71
    The services of the state governments 73
    How state governments work together 75
    How the fedeal and state governments work together 77

CHAPTER 10
The Local Governments 79
    Urban areas 80
    County governments 83
    The services of the local governments 84
    How the local governments work with the
    federal and state governments 87

Students are reading the rules for their classroom.

Chapter 1
Government and the Law

People cannot always take care of all of their needs by themselves. So people are members of groups. In a group, people can work together to take care of the needs of the members. But in every group, people are different. They have different ideas and different needs.

In order to live together peacefully, people make rules for the members of their group. The rules tell what the members can do. The rules also tell what the members cannot do. When everyone in the group obeys the rules, the members of the group can work together peacefully.

People are members of many different groups. People are members of families, neighborhoods, churches or other religious groups, towns, cities, and countries. Some groups are small, and others may be very large.

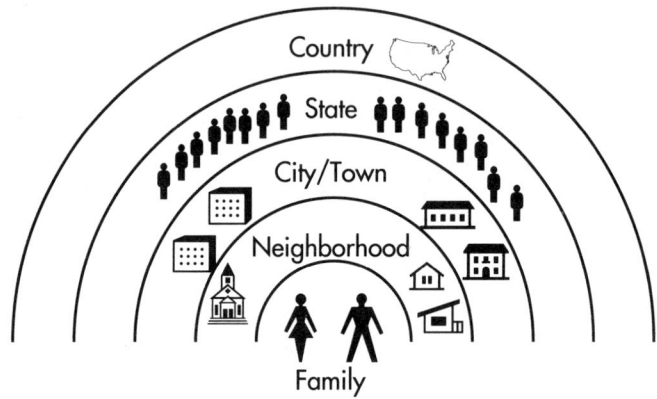

Small groups are usually part of larger groups. Families are part of neighborhoods with schools and churches. Neighborhoods are part of towns or cities. Cities belong to larger groups like states, and these groups belong to countries. Countries may also belong to larger groups. All of these groups try to take care of the needs of their members. They all need rules.

A family is a small group. A family may be made up of only two people, or many people. But even two people need rules in order to live and work together. Families usually do not write down their rules. The members of the family talk about their rules. Then everyone in the family can know about these rules and obey them.

In large groups, people may have many kinds of differences. The members may be of different races and religions. They may even speak different languages. The members of these groups also have to get along with each other. They need rules too. The members have to know about these rules. In large groups, it is usually better to write down the rules. Then everyone can know them.

What is a government?

In large groups, all the people cannot always get together to make the rules. So one person can represent other people in the group. These **representatives** make the rules for the whole group. These representatives are the government for the group.

Every country has some kind of government. One kind of government is a **democracy.** In a democracy, the people are free to vote for, or choose, the members of their government.

The government of a democracy makes rules for the people in the country. These rules are called laws. Most governments write down their laws. The government of a democracy also makes sure that people have freedom and certain **rights**. For example, in a democracy, people have the right to speak against their government.

People can speak against the government by marching in the streets.

The government of the United States is a democracy. People in the United States vote for many members of their government. These members are called representatives. In the United States, representatives make the laws for the people.

Anyone in the United States can become a representative in the government. Usually, more than one person wants to have the same job as representative. But only one person can fill each job. In a democracy, the people can vote to decide on their representative. After the people vote, the government counts the votes. One person gets the most votes. This person becomes a representative for a certain amount of time. After this time, the people vote again. Sometimes, they keep the same representative for this job. Other times, they change the representative.

Laws

In the United States, the government has many parts. But all parts of the government take care of some needs of the people. Representatives in the government make laws to take care of these needs. Other parts of the government have to carry out these laws. For example, people may need a road from one town to another town. Some people in the town may talk to some of their representatives in the government. The representatives may make a law about this new road. Then the government builds the new road.

Some laws say that the government will do certain things for the people. For example, one law says that only the federal government can print money for the United States. So a part of the government prints the money for the United States. Other laws might say that the government must give money to poor people. So another part of the government helps many poor people.

Other laws in the United States say what people cannot do. It is a crime when people break these laws. These laws about crime also tell how the government will punish lawbreakers. For example, a law about crime says that people cannot steal. If people steal things, the government can punish these lawbreakers. One part of the government tries to find the lawbreakers. Another part of the government punishes these lawbreakers.

In 1789, representatives signed the Constitution.

Chapter 2
Levels of Government in the United States

In 1789, the United States started its government. Since that time, the United States has had the same Constitution. The **Constitution** tells how the government of the United States works. The government of the United States is the government for the whole country. This government is called the **federal government**. It makes laws for all the people in the United States.

Each state also has its own constitution and its own **state government**. Each state constitution tells how the state government works. Each state government makes laws for people in its state.

In every state, there are cities and towns. Each city and town also has its own government. Each of these governments is a **local government**. Local governments make the laws for their areas in the state.

The United States has three levels of government. These levels of government are the federal, state, and local governments. Each level of government makes different laws. Each level of government takes care of the people in different ways.

Laws tell what each level of government has to do for the people. These laws tell about the services of each level of government. Other laws tell what the people have to do for each level of government. People in the United States must obey the laws of all three levels of government.

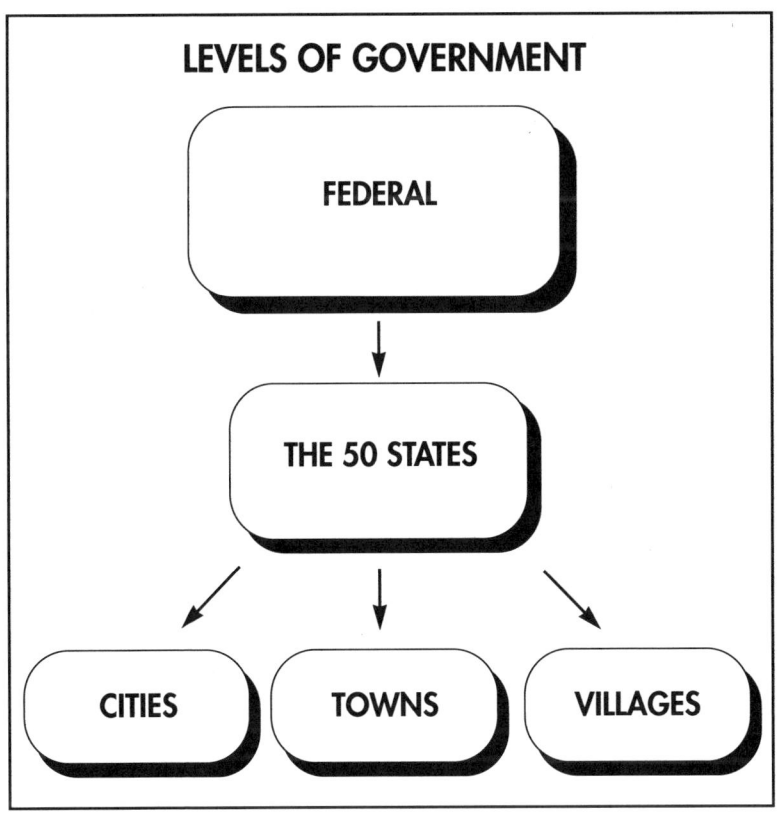

The federal government

The federal government is the government for all of the people in the United States. It is the largest level of government in the United States. It has the most power. The other levels of government often have to obey the federal government.

The Constitution says that the federal government can make laws for all the people in the United States. Federal laws may be about money, companies, taxes, wars, and the army and navy. Parts of the federal government carry out these laws.

Federal laws are about services of the federal government for the people. Some federal laws are about services for all of the people in the United States. Other federal laws tell how the federal government will help certain people at certain times. Other federal laws tell about crimes. The federal government can punish the lawbreakers of federal laws.

The federal government also must deal with the governments of other countries. Sometimes, the federal

President Bush talked to other leaders in the federal government about going to war against Iraq.

government may decide that the United States should help the government of another country. Other times, the federal government may decide that the United States will fight against another country.

The state governments

The Constitution of the United States says that the federal government can only make certain kinds of laws. It also says that a state government can only make certain kinds of laws. A state government cannot make any laws against a federal law. A state government also cannot make any laws against the Constitution.

In the United States, there are 50 states. Each state has a state government. A state government makes the laws for the people in its state. Some state laws say what the state government will do for the people in its state. Other state laws tell what people in the state must do for the state. Other state laws are about crimes in the state. The state government can punish lawbreakers of state laws.

State governments make laws about many different services. State laws may be about roads, drivers, parks, workers, companies, marriage, hospitals, and schools in the state. Parts of the state government carry out these laws. For example, a state law may say that the state government should build a hospital. So a part of the state government builds the hospital.

Each state government makes its own state laws. State governments have laws about their services. People in different states may have the same needs. So many state governments have the same kinds of services. People in different states may have different needs. So the state laws about services may be different in different states. State laws about crime also may be different in different states.

The local governments

A local government makes the laws for a small area in a state. An area may be a town, a village, or a city. Each area in a state has a local government.

The local government of a large city takes care of the needs of many people. It usually gives many services to the people in the city. Many representatives may be part of the government of a city.

Other local governments are very small. Small local governments do not have to take care of the needs of so many people. These governments usually do not give many services to the people in the area. A small local government may have only one or two representatives.

People in an area vote for representatives in their local government. The representatives in the local governments make local laws. Local laws cannot go against any state or federal laws. Some local laws are about schools, garbage, streets, police, houses, and other buildings.

Different local governments may have the same services for the people in their area. But each local government may give the service in a different way. People in each area can only get the services of their local government. These people have to obey the local laws.

For example, a local law may say that the local government will pick up the garbage from people's homes in that area. A local law in another area may say that the people have to bring their garbage to a garbage dump. The local government in this area takes care of the dump. Both local governments are giving a service to the people. Both local governments are taking care of some needs of people in the area. But each local government gives the service in a different way.

Workers for the local government use garbage trucks to pick up garbage for people in the area.

How the three levels of government work together

All three levels of American government can make laws about the same service. The laws tell how each level of government will give this service to the people. Sometimes, two or three levels of government work together to give the same service. Other times, each level of government works by itself.

Two levels of government often work together. For example, the federal government may decide that a part of the country needs a new highway. The new highway will go through more than one state. This kind of highway is called an interstate highway. The federal government has to work with each of these state governments. Together,

These signs show the way to interstate highway 17, federal highway 89A, and state highway 179.

they have to decide where they will build this new interstate highway. They also decide how they will pay for this highway.

The federal government makes a law about this new interstate highway. The federal law says that the interstate highway will go through certain states. The federal law also says that the federal government will give money to these state governments. These state governments must use this federal money to build their part of the new interstate highway. The government of these states must also use this money to take care of their part of the highway. These state governments also have to use some of their own money for the interstate highway.

Each state government may build other highways within its state. These highways may go through many local areas in the state. The state government has to work with the local government of these local areas. Together, they decide where they will build the state highway. They also decide how they will pay for the state highway. The state government and the local governments each pay a certain amount of money for the state highway. Then these governments build the state highway and take care of it.

Local governments may also decide that people in their areas need a new road. Each local government has to work with other local governments. Together, they decide where they will build this new road. They also decide how they will pay for the new road. Each local government uses its own money to build its part of the new road. Each local government takes care of its part of this road.

Workers from the local government take care of their part of the road.

Sometimes, a local government builds other roads. These roads are only in their local area. So the local government pays for these roads.

The three levels of government may work together on the same service. Sometimes, they do not have any problems working together. Other times, they have fights about the service.

The three levels of government have different amounts of power. The federal government is the strongest level of government. A state government is stronger than a local government. A state government and a local government cannot make a law against a federal law. A local government cannot make a law against a state law or a federal law.

For example, a state government may think that a certain interstate highway should not go through its state. The federal government has more power than the state government. The state government may not want to follow the plan of the federal government for the interstate highway. Then part of the federal government decides on the plan for the interstate highway. Both levels of government have to follow the plan.

Each state government builds its own state highways. Usually state highways meet the highways of other states at the state borders. The state governments may have a fight about this part of their state highway. Then a part of the federal government decides on the plan for these state highways. Both state governments have to follow this plan.

A local government may think that a certain state highway should not go through its area. But the state government has more power than the local government. The local government may not want to follow the state plan. Then a part of the state government decides on the plan for the state highway. Both levels of government have to follow the plan.

Different local governments may have fights about local roads. Part of the state government decides on the plan for these roads. The local governments have to follow the plan.

THE THREE BRANCHES OF GOVERNMENT

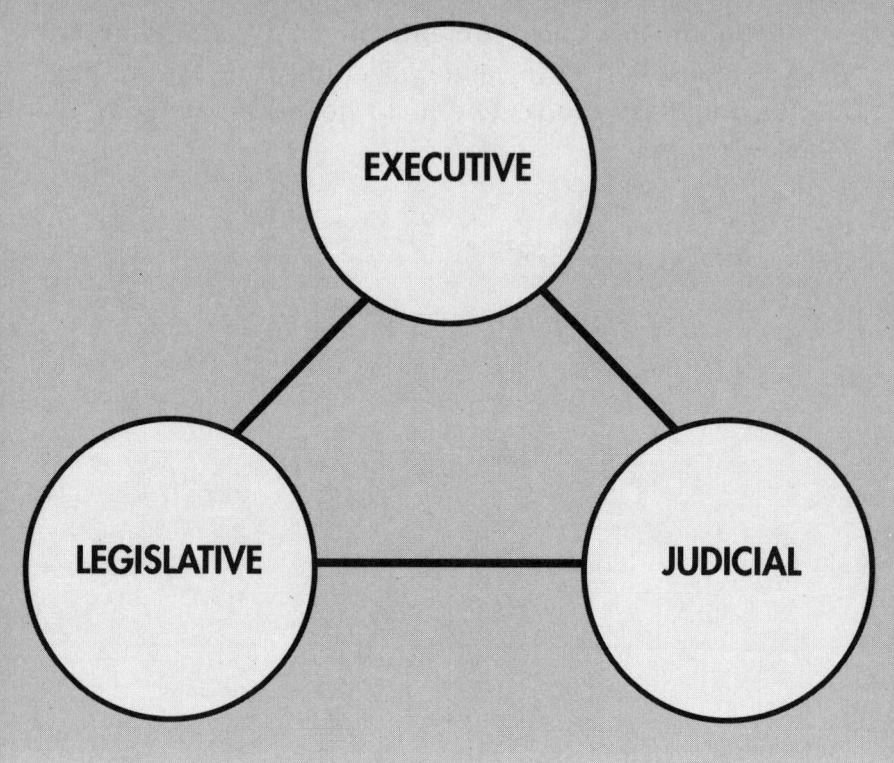

Chapter 3
The Three Branches of the Federal Government

The Constitution of the United States says that the government of the United States has three branches. One branch makes the laws for the United States. This branch is called the **legislative branch**. Another branch carries out the laws. This branch is called the **executive branch**. It also makes plans for the government of the United States. The third branch deals with lawbreakers of federal laws. It also makes sure that no law is against the Constitution. This branch is called the **judicial branch**.

The executive branch

The executive branch of the federal government is made up of the President, the Vice President, and members of the Cabinet. The President is the leader of the federal government. Americans have the right to vote for the President and the Vice President.

The President may pick many other people to work in the executive branch. Americans do not vote for these people. Some of these people work with the governments of other countries. These people are called ambassadors. Ambassadors have to think about problems in other parts of the world. Some of these problems might be war, people's rights, and trade between countries.

The President also picks people to be part of the **Cabinet**. Americans do not vote for the members of the President's Cabinet. But the Cabinet is a very important part of the executive branch.

One person in the Cabinet has to work on problems in other countries. The other people in the Cabinet have to work on certain problems in the United States. Some of these problems are about the rights of Americans, food,

President Bush is meeting with members of his Cabinet.

money, houses, and energy. The job of the members of the Cabinet is to help the President take care of these problems.

The President often meets with the members of the Cabinet. The members of the Cabinet help to make plans for the federal government. Each member of the Cabinet must help the President carry out the laws. Each member also thinks about new federal laws. These new laws might change a service of the federal government or start new service.

The President also talks to representatives in the legislative branch of the federal government. They talk about ideas for new laws. The President can ask these representatives to make certain laws. But the President cannot make a law alone. The legislative branch of the federal government has to write the federal laws.

The legislative branch

The legislative branch of the government makes the laws. **Congress** is the legislative branch of the federal government. Some federal laws tell what the federal government will do for the people in the United States. Other federal laws tell what people in the United States will have to do for the government. Many federal laws are about services in the United States. Some federal laws are about taxes. People and companies have to pay taxes to the federal government.

Congress has two parts. They are the **Senate** and the **House of Representatives**. American people vote for their representatives in both parts of Congress.

Both parts of Congress work together to make the laws of the United States. Representatives in each part of Congress may write the plan for a law. Each plan for a law is called a **bill**. Each part of Congress has to vote on

Congress has many meetings every year.

the same bill. After both parts of Congress have voted for the same bill, it may become a federal law. One part of Congress might vote for a bill. But the other part might vote against it. Then this bill will not become a new law.

The judicial branch

The federal courts make up the judicial branch of the federal government. These courts make sure that people obey the federal laws. They also make sure that each level of government obeys the Constitution.

The federal courts have to decide if a person has broken a law. In a court, some people say that a certain person has broken a law. Other people say that this person has not broken the law. These talks about this person and the law are called a case.

The federal courts decide on cases about federal laws. The federal courts also decide on cases about state laws. The federal courts listen to cases about the Constitution.

There is at least one federal court in each state. Some federal courts have more power than other federal courts.

The high courts have more power than the lower courts. Some cases can go from a lower court to a higher court.

The **Supreme Court** is the highest federal court. It has more power than any other federal court in the United States. It listens to certain cases from lower federal courts. The Supreme Court decides on these cases. No other court can listen to the cases from the Supreme Court.

All federal courts and the Supreme Court listen to cases. In some of these cases, the federal courts may have to decide if a state or federal law is against the Constitution. Then people do not have to obey this law anymore. No level of government can make this law again.

Checks and balances

The Constitution tells about the powers of the three branches of the federal government. It tells how the three branches of government have to work together. Each branch of the federal government has different powers. But no branch has more power than the other branches. Each branch makes sure that the other branches do not get too much power. Each branch checks the power of the other branches. Then one branch of the government cannot take over the other branches of the government. The Constitution set up **checks and balances** on each branch of the federal government.

Congress and the executive branch have checks on their powers. They work together to make laws. The President asks Congress to make certain laws. But Congress does not have to make these laws. Congress makes all the laws for the United States. The President must read each bill from Congress. Sometimes, the President decides that a bill should become a federal law. So the President signs the bill. Then the bill becomes a federal law. The government and all people in the United States must obey this new law.

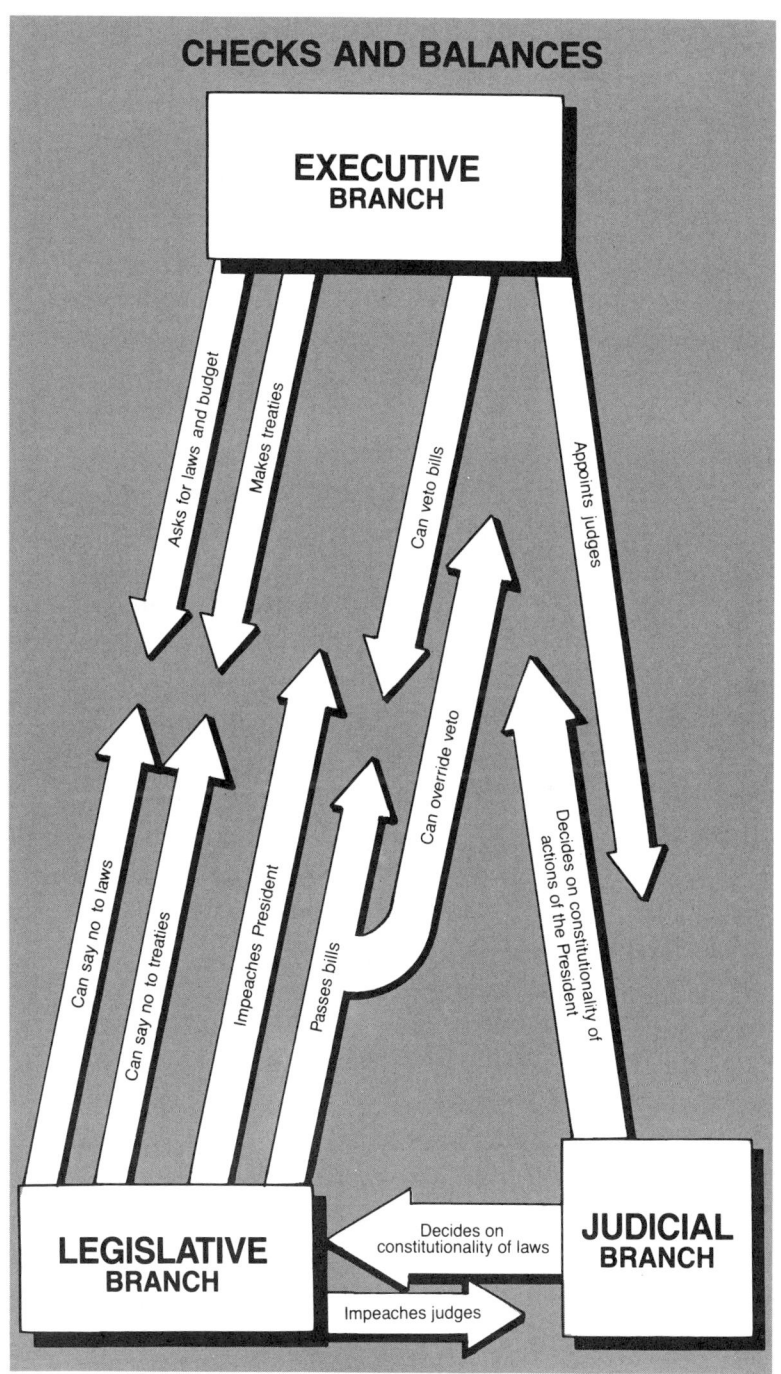

At other times, the President may think that a bill should not become a federal law. So the President does not sign the bill. The President **vetoes** it. After the President vetoes a bill, it cannot become a law at that time. But Congress may vote again about this bill. In each part of Congress, two out of every three representatives have to vote for the bill. Then it can become law. The President cannot veto this bill again. If not enough representatives vote for the bill again, the bill cannot become a federal law.

The federal courts have checks on the power of Congress. People might think that a federal law is against the Constitution. But only the federal courts can decide if a federal law is against the Constitution. Sometimes, a federal court decides that a federal law is against the Constitution. Congress might decide that the United States still needs this kind of law. So it writes a new law in a different way. The new law is about the same service. But the new law might not be against the Constitution.

The President can check the power of the judicial branch. Judges in the federal courts usually keep their jobs for the rest of their lives. But a judge may leave a job in a federal court. Then the President can pick a new judge for that court. But the President cannot tell the judges how to decide on their cases.

The Senate can check the power of the President. The Senate has to vote on each new judge for a federal court. Two out of every three Senators must vote for this person. If not enough Senators vote for this person, the President has to pick someone else for this job. Together, the President and Senators decide on the judges for federal courts. But they cannot tell these judges how to decide on the cases about federal laws.

The President also picks people for many jobs in the executive branch. Some of these people are members of the Cabinet and ambassadors to other countries. The

Senate checks this power of the President. The Senate has to vote for these ambassadors and members of the Cabinet. More than half of the Senators have to say that these people can have their new jobs. Then they can start their work. Sometimes, the Senate says that one of these people cannot have a certain job in the executive branch. Then the President has to pick another person for that job.

Congress can check other powers of the President. Congress may think that the President has broken some federal laws. Then Congress can decide that the President should not be the President any longer. Congress can try to impeach the President.

First, members of the House of Representatives must vote to have a trial for the President. More than half of the Representatives in the House have to vote for the trial. Then the Senate becomes the court for the trial. Two out of every three Senators have to vote against the President. Then the President cannot be the President any longer. The Vice President becomes the new President.

The President lives and works in the White House.

Chapter 4
The Executive Branch of the Federal Government

The executive branch of the federal government is made up of the President, Vice President, members of the Cabinet, and other people. The President is the leader of the executive branch. People in this branch make plans for the federal government. Some plans are about the services of the federal government. The federal government has these services for the people in the United States. Other plans are about the United States and other countries.

The Constitution says that the United States will always have a President and a Vice President. If the President dies, then the Vice President becomes the President. If Congress impeaches the President, the Vice President becomes the President.

The Constitution also says that the American people can vote for the President and Vice President every four years. The American people cannot vote for the other people in the executive branch. The President picks these people. These people help the President. Some of these people are part of the Cabinet.

The President

Every four years, the American people vote for the President. The person with the most votes becomes the President. Sometimes, the American people **elect** the same president for four more years. Other times, a different person becomes the President. But the American people cannot elect the same President for more than eight years.

On television, George Bush and Bill Clinton talk to people about electing the President.

The President has to know about all of the problems in the United States. Some services of the federal government try to take care of these problems. The President makes plans for the services of the federal government. The President talks to Congress about plans for these services. For example, the President may think that the federal government should give more help to poor people in the United States. So the President talks to Congress about new laws. These laws would give more services to poor people.

President Kennedy spoke to Congress about the government of the United States.

The President also has to know about the problems in the world. The President has to decide what the United States should do about these problems. Then the President makes plans about some services of the federal government for other countries. For example, a country in Africa might not be able to grow enough food for all of its people. The President talks to Congress about the problem. Congress might make a law about a service for this country in Africa. Then the federal government sends food to this country.

The President is the leader of the executive branch. So the President has to make plans for services for the many, many people in the United States. The President also has to make plans for American services for other countries. The plans of the President can change the services of the federal government in the United States.

The plans of the President can also change the services of the federal government for other countries in the world. For example, the President can decide that the United States should help the government of another country. So the President might send soldiers and money to that country.

The Vice President

The Vice President knows about the President's plans. The Vice President often talks to the President and other people in the executive branch. The Vice President also talks to members of Congress. In these talks, the Vice President tries to help the President.

The Vice President has to know about problems in the United States and in other parts of the world. The Vice President visits different parts of the United States. The Vice President talks to leaders of different groups and gets information from these leaders. Then the Vice President tells the President about the ideas of these groups.

The Vice President also visits other parts of the world. The Vice President talks with the leaders of other countries. The Vice President tells these leaders about the plans of the United States. These leaders tell the Vice President about the plans of their countries. The Vice President tells the President about the talks with these leaders. In this way, the President can learn more about the plans of the governments of other countries. Then the President can talk with the leaders. Together, they can all make better plans for the United States and these countries.

The Cabinet

A special group of people in the executive branch helps the President. This group is called the Cabinet. Each member of the Cabinet is a leader of one part of the executive branch. Each part is called a department. The leader of each department is called a **Secretary**. The Secretary of each department is a member of the Cabinet.

Each Secretary has a lot of power. Each Secretary makes plans for one department. Each Secretary decides on how the department should spend its money.

Each Secretary helps the President with one department. For example, one department in the Cabinet is called the Department of Defense.

This department protects the United States from armies of other countries. The army, navy, air force, and marines are part of this department. The Secretary of Defense talks to the President about plans to make the United States strong. They may talk about problems with other countries, democracy, war, weapons, and peace.

There are fourteen departments in the Cabinet. Some Secretaries talk to the President about problems in the United States. Then the President decides on how the federal government will deal with these problems in the United States. Other Secretaries talk to the President about problems in the world. Then the President decides on how the United States will deal with problems in other parts of the world.

DEPARTMENTS IN THE CABINET

DEPARTMENT   SERVICES OF THE DEPARTMENT

Agriculture ....Helps farmers
Takes care of food stamps

Commerce.....................Helps people in companies
Takes care of trade between companies

Defense..........................Runs the army, navy, and air force
Makes plans for war

Education.....................Makes rules for public schools
Gives money to public schools

Energy ....Makes plans for fuel
Sells electricity from federal dams

Health and Human......Takes care of Social Security programs
Services   Makes sure that foods are safe

Housing and Urban ......Helps to build homes in the cities
Development   Lends money to people for houses

Interior..........................Runs federal parks
Takes care of water services

Justice............................Takes care of federal courts and prisons
Finds lawbreakers of federal laws

Labor ....Makes rules for workers
Runs services to help people get jobs

State...............................Watches over the United States
and other countries
Makes treaties with other countries

Transportation..............Takes care of federal highways
Makes rules for airplanes, cars
and trains

Treasury........................Takes care of money in the United States

Veterans Affairs...........Takes care of people who were
once in the armed services

The United States has many large farms. The Secretary of Agriculture helps to make sure that farmers grow the right amount of food for the United States and other countries.

The American people do not elect the members of the Cabinet. The President picks one person to be the Secretary of each department. Then the Senate has to vote about each Secretary. The members of the Senate must decide if each Secretary will do a good job. The Senate can vote against this person. Then the President has to pick a different person for this job.

The President might decide that a Secretary is not doing a good job. Then the President can take the job away from this Secretary. But the Senate itself cannot take a job away from any member of the Cabinet.

The Secretaries give a lot of information about their departments to the President. The President talks with each Secretary about plans for the services of that department. The President uses this information to make plans for the federal government.

The members of the Cabinet also give important information to members of Congress. This information is about their departments. A Secretary may think that the United States needs a new law about a service. The Secretary thinks that the law will help to end certain problems. So the Secretary tells some members of Congress about the need for the new law. Then these members of Congress might write a bill. This Secretary might also speak at meetings of Congress about this bill. At these meetings, the Secretary can say why the United States needs this new law.

The President and Congress

The President and Congress work together in many ways. The President makes the plans for the United States. But the President alone cannot make the laws. The Congress is the legislative branch of the federal government. The legislative branch has to make laws for these plans.

The President often talks to members of Congress about certain new laws. These laws are about services and money for the federal government. Many times, members of Congress try to make these new laws. Other times, members of Congress do not try to make these new laws.

The President has to make a special plan about the money of the federal government. This plan is called the federal budget. The federal **budget** talks about the cost of each service of the federal government. It also tells about tax money and how the government will pay for these services.

The President has to write a new budget every year. The President talks to the members of Congress about the budget. The President must think about all of the services of the federal government. Some of these services are for people in the United States. Other services of the federal government are for other countries. The President thinks about the cost of each service. The President also has to think about tax money and how the United States will pay for these services.

The President talks to the members of the Cabinet. They talk about the federal budget for each of the departments. The President might decide that the federal government should spend a lot of money for one service. Then that part of the budget would be bigger than other parts. The President might decide that the federal government should not spend a lot of money for another service. Then that part of the budget may be smaller than other parts.

President Reagan gave a book about the federal budget to the leader of each part of Congress.

The President has to send the budget to Congress. Then Congress thinks about all the parts of the federal budget. The President and Congress may have many meetings about the budget. Members of Congress may decide to change parts of the budget. Congress has to vote for the federal budget. Then the federal government has to follow the budget. Congress writes bills about services and money of the federal government.

The President also has to think about the services of the United States for other countries. These services are also part of the federal budget. The President and leaders of other countries may decide that their countries need a **treaty**. A treaty tells what each country will do for the other country.

The President may think that the United States should obey a certain treaty. But the President cannot decide that the United States will obey a treaty. The Senate has to vote about the treaty. Sometimes, the Senate votes for the treaty. Then the United States has to obey the treaty. Other times, the Senate votes against a treaty. Then the President cannot make the United States obey the treaty.

In 1978, President Carter signed a treaty with the leaders of the governments of Israel and Egypt.

The members of Congress work in this building.

Chapter 5
The Legislative Branch of the Federal Government

The legislative branch of the federal government is the Congress. The two parts of Congress are the Senate and the House of Representatives. Together, they make the federal laws. Everyone in the United States has to obey these laws.

The American people vote for the members of both parts of Congress. Each member of Congress is a representative for people in certain parts of the United States. Each member of Congress tries to know about the needs of these people. Then each member of Congress can try to make laws about services to help these people.

The Senate

The Constitution says that each state must have two Senators in the Senate. There are 50 states in the United States. So the Senate is made up of 100 Senators.

Senators are elected to their jobs for six years. During this time, the Senators help to make laws for all Americans. They talk to the people about federal laws. People can talk to their Senators about their ideas about federal laws. Sometimes, a Senator will try to make a new law. Other times, a Senator will try to change an old law. Senators try to do a good job for the people in their state. If the Senators do a good job, people in their state will elect them again. Then these Senators can keep their jobs for six more years.

The Vice President is the leader of the Senate. The Vice President is not a Senator. But one of the jobs of the Vice President is to lead the meetings of the Senate. There are many meetings during the year.

At some meetings, members of the Senate talk about a bill. At other meetings, they have to vote about a bill. Sometimes, the vote is a tie. Then the Vice President votes about this bill. This vote breaks the tie.

The House of Representatives

The Constitution says that every state in the United States must have at least one Representative in the House of Representatives. Sometimes, the House of Representatives is called the House.

A federal law says that the House must have one Representative for about every 550,000 people in the United States. These people live in one area of a state. These areas are called **Congressional districts**. There are 435 Congressional districts in the United States. The

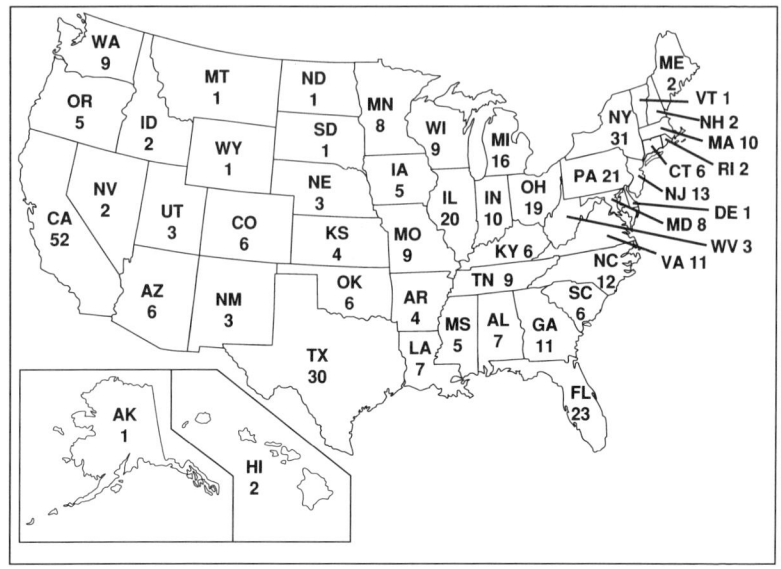

The number of Representatives of the House from each state.

people in each district elect one Representative to the House. So there are 435 Representatives in the House.

Most states have many districts. So these states have many Representatives in the House. For example, one state might have 52 districts. Each of these districts has about 550,000 people. So this state has 52 Representatives in the House. Other states may have only one district. There can be less than 550,000 people in these states. But these states must have one Representative.

The Representatives in the House are elected to their jobs for two years. During the two years, the Representatives make laws for all Americans. But they have to know about the needs of the people in their district. Then the Representatives can try to make laws about services to help these people. If the Representative does a good job, the people in the district will vote for him or her again. Then these Representatives can keep their jobs for two more years.

The House of Representatives has many meetings during the year. The Representatives do a lot of work at these meetings. They talk about bills, rewrite them, and vote about them.

In the House of Representatives, the members elect one Representative to be the leader of the House. This Representative is called the Speaker of the House. This person has more power than any other Representative in the House. At each meeting, the Speaker decides what bills the House will talk about. The Speaker also decides when the Representatives will vote on certain bills. Representatives can only talk at a meeting of the House when the Speaker calls on them.

How a bill becomes a law

The Senate and the House of Representatives work together to make the laws. Members of each part of Congress can decide that the United States needs a new law. So they write a bill. Sometimes, a bill starts in the House of Representatives. More than half of the Representatives have to vote for the bill. Then the bill goes to the Senate.

Other times, a bill starts in the Senate. More than half of the Senators have to vote for the bill. Then the bill goes to the House.

Each part of Congress has to vote for the same bill. If both parts of Congress pass the bill, it may become a federal law.

It may take a long time for a bill to become a law. Many bills never become laws. All bills have to follow certain steps. Some bills cannot go to the next step.

These steps show how a bill from the House of Representatives can become a law. A bill from the Senate would have to follow the same steps.

1. A Representative talks to other Representatives about a service of the federal government. They decide that the federal government needs a new law for the service.

2. Representatives in the House may write a bill about the service. They have to write the bill in a special way. Then other members of the House of Representatives read the bill and think about it. They decide if the United States needs the new law.

3. The bill goes to one of the special groups of Representatives in the House. These special groups are called committees. Every Representative is a member of at least one of the committees in the House. Each committee works on many different bills about the same service. A committee might deal with one of these bills for a long time. The members of the committee might write the bill in many different ways. Then the members of the committee decide on one bill and vote for it.

4. The committee might decide that the whole House of Representatives should think about the bill. Some members of the committee talk to the Speaker of the House about the bill. The Speaker decides when the whole House will talk about the bill.

5. The Speaker decides that all of the members of the House can talk about the bill. Some of the Representatives say that they like the bill. Other members of House tell why they do not like the bill. Some Representatives may want to change some parts of the bill.

6. The bill goes back to the same committee. Then this committee talks about the bill again. Members of the committee change a part of the bill. Then the committee votes for the bill and sends it back to the House.

7. The whole House has to talk about the bill again. The Representatives in the House vote about the bill. More than half of the Representatives in the House have to vote for the bill. Then members of the House can send the bill to the Senate.

8. The leader of the Senate sends the bill to one of the committees in the Senate. The members of this committee talk about the bill. Then the committee votes for the bill and sends it to the Senate.

9. The members of the Senate talk about the bill. Then they can decide to vote about the bill. More than half of the Senators have to vote for the bill. Then Congress can send the bill to the President.

10. Sometimes, the House and the Senate pass bills about the same service. These bills are almost the same. But one part of one bill may be a little different from one part of another bill. So Senators and Representatives have to make these two bills into one bill. They write a new bill. The new bill is a lot like the two other bills. The Senate and the House each have to vote for the new bill. Then the bill can go to the President.

Some members of the Foreign Relations Committee in the Senate talk about a bill.

11. The President has to think about the bill. If the President signs the bill, it becomes a law. Then all people in the United States have to obey the new law.

12. If the President decides to veto the bill, Congress can vote about the bill again. In each part of the Congress, two out of three members have to vote for the bill. Then the bill can become a law. If not enough members of Congress vote for the bill again, this bill cannot become a law.

Congress and the American people

Members of Congress are Representatives for people in different districts in the United States. The members of Congress are supposed to know about the needs of the people in their districts. Members of Congress talk to these people. They try to find out what new laws would help these people. The members of Congress also try to find out if some federal laws could hurt the people in their district.

Sometimes, people talk to members of Congress about their ideas for a bill. Then the members of Congress may try to pass these bills. For example, there are many farms in Iowa. Sometimes, farmers from Iowa talk to their members of Congress about problems on their farms. Then these representatives in Congress try to make laws about land and farmers. These laws will help the farmers in Iowa. These laws may also help farmers in other states.

It usually takes a long time for a bill to become a law. During this time, people can read about the bill in newspapers and magazines. They can talk to many other people about the bill. They may also talk to members of Congress about the bill. They can tell representatives what they think about the bill. People may ask a representative to vote for a bill or against a bill. Information from the people helps members of Congress to decide about their vote on a bill.

People in the United States can give their ideas to members of Congress in many different ways. They can call the members of Congress on the telephone. They can write letters to them. They can visit members of Congress in their offices.

Representative Ronald Dellums of California reads his mail from people in the United States.

All representatives in a democracy have to win elections to keep their jobs. Members of Congress listen to the people. When representatives vote on bills, they have to think about the people in their Congressional district. They have to decide if most of these people want this bill.

Most of the time, members of Congress want to keep their jobs. So before the election, each representative must talk to many people. Each representative must try to win the vote of the people in the Congressional district. The things people do to win an election are called a **campaign**.

Carol Moseley Braun became the Senator from Illinois.

Every few years, representatives must spend time on their campaign. They have to make sure that many people in their district know about their ideas and their work in Congress. Usually, campaigns cost a lot of money.

People, companies, and other groups can give money to the campaign of any representative. This money is called a **campaign contribution**. Representatives use this money to put ads on TV and in newspapers. Representatives may also use this money to travel and talk to people or to pay workers in the campaign. All of these things may help to win the election.

Every person in the United States can also join special groups. There are many kinds of special groups. Usually, the members of each group have the same ideas about a certain service of the federal government. So each group wants the federal government to make certain laws about that service. Members of each group think that certain laws will make the service better.

For example, one group may want the federal government to keep federal parks cleaner. Members of this group may want certain laws about parks. These laws would make sure that the federal government kept the federal parks clean. Another group may not think that the federal government should spend so much money on parks. Members of this group do not want the same laws about parks as the other group. Each group talks to members of Congress. Each group is speaking for many people. So each group has more power than one person. Each group can tell members of Congress that they should vote for certain bills. The members of Congress listen to these groups. Then they decide on bills about federal parks.

Sometimes, a special group hires a person to talk to members of Congress. This person is called a **lobbyist**. Lobbyists tell representatives what their group would like Congress to do. Talking to representatives in the government in this way is called **lobbying**. Years ago, lobbyists sometimes talked to members of Congress in the lobby of the Senate or the House. This is how the job got its name.

Lobbyists not only talk to representatives. They also may give campaign contributions to representatives. Sometimes, campaign contributions from lobbyists are very large. There are federal laws about campaign contributions. These laws say that lobbyists cannot give more than a certain amount of money to one representative. But this money may make the representative think more about the lobbyists and what they want. Some people think that there should be stronger laws about these kinds of campaign contributions.

At times, members of Congress think that they need more information about a certain bill. So members of each part of Congress have special meetings about the bills. These meetings may take place in many different cities and towns in the United States. Anyone may go to these meetings. At these meetings, people can talk to members of Congress about the bill. Lobbyists can also talk about the bill.

After these meetings, the members of Congress have a lot of information. They can use this information to decide on how to vote on the bill.

The Supreme Court building in Washington, DC.

Chapter 6
The Judicial Branch of the Federal Government

The judicial branch of the federal government is made up of the federal courts. These courts decide on cases about federal laws. In some cases, the federal courts decide if a person has broken a federal law. In other cases, these courts deal with cases about people's rights.

Judges in federal courts cannot make laws. They also cannot ask Congress to make certain kinds of laws. Federal judges have to study all American laws and the cases about these laws. Judges have to think about the meaning of each law. The judges use this meaning when they decide on a case.

Judges in the federal courts listen to two kinds of cases. One kind of case is about crime. These cases are called criminal cases. In these cases, the federal courts decide how the federal government will punish the lawbreaker. The other kind of case is about fights between people or companies. These cases are called civil cases. In these cases, the federal courts decide how the people in the case should end the fight.

There are lower and higher federal courts. In some cases, the people may think that they did not have a fair trial in the lower court. They can ask a higher court to listen to their case. They have to listen to the higher court.

The highest federal court is the Supreme Court. The Supreme Court listens to civil cases and criminal cases. No court in the United States has more power than the Supreme Court.

Cases in federal courts

The lower federal courts have trials for many different cases. Some of these cases are about federal laws. Other cases are about state laws. The highest state courts have already listened to these cases. Then the lower federal courts may listen to these cases.

Cases about federal laws start in the lowest federal court. The lower federal court may decide that people have broken a law. But these people may not think that they have had a fair trial. So they ask a higher federal court to listen to their case. In some cases, the higher court says that it will not listen to the case. Then the people have to listen to the lower court. In other cases, the higher court says that the Supreme Court will listen to the case. Then the Supreme Court decides about the case.

Some cases in the federal courts are about state laws and the Constitution. In each state, there are lower and higher courts. State courts work like the federal courts. Cases about state laws start in the lowest state court. These cases can go to the highest state court. The highest state court may decide on these cases. But the people in the case may still not think that they had a fair trial in the state court. So they ask the lowest federal court to listen to their case.

Some cases in the federal courts are about the Constitution and local, state, or federal laws. The federal courts have to decide if any law is against the Constitution. These cases may start in a local, state, or federal court. Sometimes, the federal courts say that a law is not against the Constitution. Then people obey this law. Other times, the federal courts say that a law is against the Constitution. Then the government cannot use this law.

Other cases in the federal courts are about people's rights and the Constitution. In these cases, people may think that someone has taken away their rights. The Constitution says that no person can take these rights away from people. One of these rights is the right to speak about anything. For example, a company might make a rule for its workers. This rule might say that at the company, the workers cannot talk against the company. The workers can take the company to court because the company will not let them have this right. Different state and federal courts might listen to the case about the workers and the company. Then the federal courts have to decide if the company has taken away rights from the workers. The company and the workers have to listen to the federal court.

The Supreme Court

The Supreme court is the highest court in the United States. It has the most power. The Supreme Court listens to cases from other federal courts. It also listens to certain cases from state courts. After the Supreme Court has decided about a case, no other court can listen to the case. Both sides of the case have to listen to the Supreme Court.

The Supreme Court is made up of nine judges. Sometimes, one of the judges dies or leaves this job. Then the President can pick a new judge for the Supreme Court. The Senate must vote for every new judge in the Supreme Court. Then these judges can have their jobs for the rest of their lives.

The judges on the Supreme Court have to know the Constitution and study many different laws and cases. Sometimes, they listen to a case about a certain law. They have to know all about this law. They have to decide on the meaning of the law in the case. They may decide that this law is against the Constitution. Then the government

The nine justices in the Supreme Court in 1992.

cannot use this law anymore. In this way, the Supreme Court decides on the meaning of the Constitution. Judges in all other courts have to think about the Constitution in the same way as the Supreme Court.

For example, some students in a public school broke many rules of the school. The school did not have a meeting with these students. The school just said that these students could not come back to school for many days. The students thought that the school had taken away their rights. So they hired a lawyer.

In court, the lawyer for the students said that the school had not obeyed the Constitution. The school had not given the students their rights because the school did not have a meeting with these students. At this meeting, people from the school and these students could have talked. They could have spoken about the school rules, the events in the school, and the punishment. Then after this meeting, the school could have punished the students. But the school did not listen to their side of the case. The school just punished the students. The school did not give the students the right to speak about these events.

Different state and federal courts listened to this case. In 1975, the Supreme Court listened to this case. The Supreme Court said that the school had not obeyed part of the Constitution. This part of the Constitution is the 14th Amendment. It says that all people in the United States have certain rights. The Supreme Court said that students in a public school must get their rights. The people from the school should have had a special meeting for these students. Then the school could have punished the students.

Today, all public schools have to use this meaning of the 14th Amendment to the Constitution. All public schools have to make sure that students get all of their rights.

This is the Constitution of the United States.

Chapter 7
The Legislative Branch and the Constitution

The 1787, the writers of the Constitution thought that the United States should always have the same Constitution. But they knew that life in the United States would change after many, many years. They wanted to make sure that the Constitution could change, too. So the writers of the Constitution wrote two special parts of the Constitution.

One special part of the Constitution says that the Congress can write new parts to the Constitution. These new parts are called **amendments**. An amendment can change any part of the Constitution. An amendment can also make sure that people have certain rights. After an amendment becomes part of the Constitution, the Constitution is different, No level of government can make a law against this amendment. No level of government can use some of its old laws. These laws are now against the Constitution.

The other special part of the Constitution says that Congress can write many different federal laws. But these laws have to help the federal government to do its work. As the needs of the United States change, Congress can change the laws. But these laws cannot be against the Constitution.

How amendments become part of the Constitution

The Constitution tells how a new amendment can become part of the Constitution. Parts of the federal and state governments always have to follow these steps. Here are the steps.

1. Members of Congress think about the laws of the United States and the Constitution. Congress may think that the Constitution does not take care of some needs of the American people. Congress may also think that a federal law may not be able to take care of these needs. So members of Congress decide that a new amendment should become part of the Constitution.

2. A new amendment can start in the Senate or the House of Representatives. Senators or Representatives might write the new amendment. Then each part of Congress has to vote on the amendment. In each part of Congress, two out of every three members must vote for the amendment. Both parts of Congress have to pass the amendment.

3. Congress sends the amendment to the legislative branch of each state government. The legislative branch has to decide if it should vote about the amendment. In some state governments, the legislative branch does not vote about the amendment. In other state governments, the legislative branch decides that they should vote about the amendment.

4. The legislative branches of many state governments decide that they will vote about the new amendment. Three out of every four states have to vote for the amendment. Then the amendment can become part of the Constitution.

The amendments to the Constitution

In 1791, the first ten amendments became part of the Constitution. These amendments are called the **Bill of Rights**. Each of these amendments says that the government must give certain rights to all Americans. The government can never take these rights away. For example, the 1st Amendment says that people can belong to any kind of church. So no government can make people be members of a certain church.

Since that date, only 16 other amendments have become part of the Constitution. So today there are 26 amendments to the Constitution. Some of these amendments changed certain things about the federal government. For example, the 22nd Amendment says that American people cannot elect the same President more than twice. Other amendments make sure that Americans have certain rights. For example, the 15th Amendment is about voters. No government can say that people cannot vote because of the color of their skin.

In 1977, people showed the federal government that they wanted the 27th Amendment to become part of the Constitution.

Each amendment must follow the same steps. Then it may become part of the Constitution. At times, Congress and enough of the state governments pass a new amendment. Then the amendment becomes part of the Constitution. Other times, Congress passes an amendment. But not enough state governments pass it. This amendment does not become part of the Constitution.

For example, in the 1970s, Congress passed an amendment about women's rights. This amendment would make sure that women would have the same rights as men. But this new amendment did not become part of the Constitution.

In 1971, the House of Representatives passed this new amendment. In 1972, the Senate also passed this amendment. Then the legislative branch of the state governments had to vote about this amendment. By 1982, many state governments had said that the 27th Amendment should be part of the Constitution. But not enough state governments voted for this amendment. So the 27th Amendment did not become part of the Constitution.

Laws and the Supreme Court

Each level of government tries to make sure that their laws are not against the Constitution. Judges in the Supreme Court listen to cases about laws and the Constitution. In these cases, the judges have to decide if any American law is against the Constitution. The judges in the Supreme Court have to think about the meaning of the law in the case. They also have to think about the meaning of the Constitution. In some cases, the Supreme Court decides that a law is against the Constitution. Then no level of government can use that law.

Sometimes, some Representatives may not like the way

that the Supreme Court decided on the meaning of the Constitution. But these Representatives have to use this same meaning of the Constitution when they write bills.

For example, in 1933, Congress passed a law about farmers. The law said that the federal government would pay farmers to grow less food. In 1936, the judges in the Supreme Court listened to a case about this federal law. The Supreme Court decided that some parts of this law

Before 1964, some state laws said that African-Americans could not use the same places as white people.

were against the Constitution. So the federal government could not use the law anymore.

Some members of Congress thought that the federal government should still help farmers. So they wrote another bill to help farmers. Congress passed this new law. The courts never said that any part of this new law was against the Constitution.

The Supreme Court can also say that a law is not against the Constitution. For example, in 1964, the federal government passed a law about African-Americans. This law is called the Civil Rights Act. One part of this law says that African-Americans have the same rights as white Americans.

In 1964, an African-American tried to rent a room in a hotel in Atlanta, Georgia. The hotel would not let this African-American stay there. This African-American thought that the owners of the hotel were breaking the federal law. The owners of the hotel thought that the Civil Rights Act was against the Constitution. Different federal courts listened to the case between the African-American and the owners of the hotel.

In 1964, the Supreme Court listened to this case. The judges of the Supreme Court said that the owners of the hotel were breaking a federal law. The owners of the hotel had to let people of any race rent a room in their hotel.

In this case, the Supreme Court said that the Civil Rights Act was not against the Constitution. The federal government could make people obey this federal law.

People's rights and the Supreme Court

Many amendments to the Constitution are about the rights of people. No American government can ever take these rights away from people in the United States. Sometimes, people may think that a part of the government has taken away one of their rights. These people can take the government to court. The Supreme Court may listen to this case because it is about the Constitution and people's rights. In one of these cases, the Supreme Court may decide on a new meaning of an amendment. Then all levels of government have to use this meaning of the amendment.

For example, the 5th Amendment says that the government can never make people talk against themselves. People have these rights when the police ask them questions about a crime. People on trial also have the same rights.

In 1963, police in Arizona thought that Ernesto Miranda had broken a state law. The police said that Miranda had raped a woman. They brought him to the police station. They asked him questions about the crime. Miranda answered the questions. The police wrote down his answers on a paper. He did not know about his rights. Then the police asked him to sign the paper. Miranda signed it. Later, the state government had a trial about this crime.

Ernesto Miranda talked to his lawyer about his case.

At this trial, the state government talked about Miranda's answers to the police. These answers helped the state government to show that Miranda had broken the law. The state court decided that Miranda had to go to jail.

Miranda's lawyer did not think that the state government had a fair trial for Miranda. The lawyer thought that the police should have told Miranda about his rights and the 5th Amendment. Miranda did not know that he did not have to speak to the police about the crime.

After the trial, Miranda's lawyer decided to take Miranda's case to another state court. Other state courts and federal courts listened to this case.

In 1966, the Supreme Court listened to the case about Miranda. It said that Miranda had not gotten all of his rights. The police had not obeyed the 5th Amendment. If the police had told Miranda about his rights, then they could have asked him questions about the crime.

In the Miranda case, the Supreme Court also decided on a new meaning of the 5th Amendment. The Supreme Court said that people always have rights. When the police ask people questions about crimes, the people have rights. People do not always have to answer these questions. People can always talk to a lawyer before they talk to the police. During these talks with the lawyer, people can decide about their answers to the police. Then they may answer the questions.

All police have to know about Miranda's case. The police always have to tell people about their rights when they question people about a crime.

President Bush and the President of the Soviet Union, Mikhael Gorbachev, talked about ending the Cold War.

Chapter 8
The United States As a World Power

Some countries in the world are very rich. So the governments of these countries are very strong and powerful. These governments have large armies, navies, and air forces. These armed forces make sure that other governments cannot take over their country. They protect their government and the people. In rich and powerful countries, most of the people have enough food. They can live well. The governments of these countries usually give many services to the people.

The United States is one of the most powerful countries in the world. Until 1991, there was another very powerful country. It was called the Soviet Union.

The Soviet Union was made up of many different, smaller countries. These countries were called Republics. The Republics were like the states in the United States. The government of the Soviet Union had a lot of power over these Republics. The Republics had to obey the government of the Soviet Union.

In 1991, big changes took place in the Soviet Union. The people wanted better lives. But the government could not help them. The government started to fall apart. The Republics started to set up their own governments. They did not always have to listen to the Soviet Union any more.

The largest Republic is called Russia. The new government of Russia is not the same kind of government as the old Soviet Union. Russia is not as powerful as the old Soviet Union. It does not have much power over the other Republics. The new government of Russia is too weak to start a war against the United States.

The United States is a rich and powerful country. It has a strong government. Other countries in the world also are rich and powerful. For example, the governments of Germany and Japan are also very strong. But many other countries in the world are not very rich and powerful. These countries cannot give a lot of services to their people. Often the people in these countries are very poor. They may not have enough food to eat. Some of these countries are called the **Third World** countries.

Different kinds of government

Each country in the world has a government. The government of the United States is a democracy. The governments of many other countries are democracies, too. In a democracy, people elect representatives in their government. These representatives make the laws for the people. Democratic governments make sure that people always have certain rights.

In a democracy, people have the right to talk about their ideas about government. Some groups of people have the same ideas about their government. These people become members of the same political party. In a democracy, there may be many political parties. Each representative is a member of one political party. During elections, people can vote and change their representatives.

In a democracy, people can own companies. These companies make things for people or give services to people. The governments of democratic countries also give many services to people.

Some other countries are not democracies. In these countries, most people cannot elect the members of their government. A few people make the laws for all of the people. But all of the people have to obey the laws. The governments in these countries do not let people have many rights.

In some countries, the government is a **communist government**. China and Cuba still have communist governments. The government of the Soviet Union was a communist government. In this kind of government, there is only one political party. It is the **Communist Party**. Only members of the Communist Party can be part of the government. In communist countries, people do not have as many rights as people in democracies. The government of communist countries owns all of the companies in that country. People cannot own their own companies. All workers work for the government.

Now there are fewer communist governments in the world. Many countries in Eastern Europe used to have communist governments. Now they are more democratic.

Russia and the other Republics used to have communist governments. Now they are more democratic, too. More and more countries in the world are becoming more democratic.

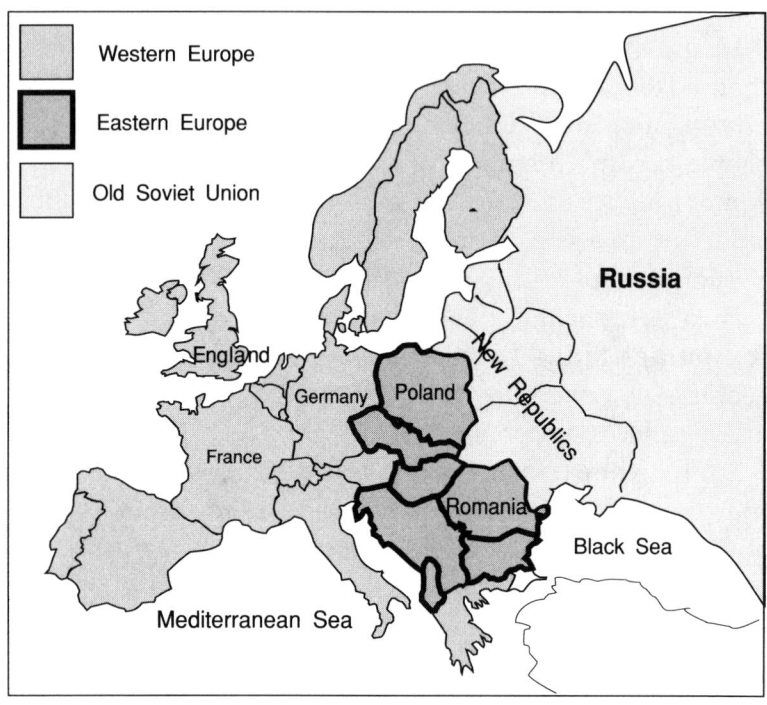

In some countries the army runs the government. In other countries, one strong person has most of the power. This person is called a **dictator**. In these countries, people often do not have the right to elect the members of their government. But this government still makes the laws for the people. The governments in these countries do not let people have many rights. But these governments usually let the people run their own companies.

Different Third World countries may have different kinds of governments. In some of these countries, the government may be a democracy. A political party, or the army, or a dictator may run the government in other Third World countries.

The United States and other countries

Before the changes in the Soviet Union, the United States and the Soviet Union had very different ideas about how governments should work. These two powerful countries were enemies. They knew that their fights could turn into another world war. Countries with democratic governments were usually friendly toward the United States. Countries with communist governments were usually friendly toward the Soviet Union.

The United States wanted more Third World countries to be friendly toward the United States. Some of these countries were democracies. Others did not have democratic governments. The United States hoped that these countries would become democracies. They could help the United States in a war against the Soviet Union.

The Soviet Union wanted more Third World countries to be on their side in a war against the United States. So the Soviet Union also helped certain Third World countries. The Soviet Union wanted these countries to have communist governments. They could help the Soviet Union in a war against the United States.

Since 1991, the United States and the new government in Russia have become more alike. More and more, they have the same ideas about how governments should work. They have some of the same problems. Sometimes, they work together to help poorer countries.

The United States and the government in Russia now worry more about their own people. Both governments try to give their people enough services. This can be a problem in both countries. But in Russia, it is a much bigger problem. Both the United States and Russia worry about Third World countries. They do not want these countries to start wars with one another. Some of these poor countries have very big problems. Sometimes, they cannot get enough food for all their people. These countries may not be good neighbors with other poor counties. In some of these countries, the governments do not help their people to have a better life. The leaders of these countries want power and money for themselves.

There is a special problem with the new government in Russia. The other countries from the old Soviet Union have the same problem. All of these countries once had communist governments. These communist governments did not run the countries well. These countries did not have modern ways of making things or giving services to people. Companies in these countries were owned by the government. These companies did not make things very well.

Most of the people in these countries now watch TV. They can see how people live in the United States. They want to live like this, too. They know that people in the United States have better lives than they do. The differences sometimes make them angry about their governments.

The United States wants the new governments in Russia and Eastern Europe to become strong democracies. The United States does not want these smaller countries to fight against each other. The United States also does not want the people in the smaller countries to fight among themselves. Fights could break these counties up into even smaller countries.

Before 1991, the United States and the Soviet Union thought that they might someday have a war. This time was called the Cold War. Now the Cold War is over. The chance of a war between the United States and Russia is very small. But the United States worries about the bombs and weapons that are still in some parts of the old Soviet Union. Talks between the United States and the new government in Russia have helped to make these fears smaller.

People from the government of the United States and the

governments in Russia and the new countries have decided to get rid of many of the bombs and weapons. The leaders of these countries talk about how to do this. They decide what each country will do. Then they write a treaty. Leaders of governments sign the treaty and say that they will obey them. In the United States, the President signs the treaty. But the Senate has to vote for it, too. Then the government of the United States has to obey the treaty.

During the Cold War, President Nixon signed a treaty about weapons in the United States and the Soviet Union.

The government of the United States has treaties with the governments of many different countries. For example, the United States has treaties with England, France, Germany, and Japan. Many of these treaties are about trade. More and more, the United States and other countries see themselves as a big family. The members of this world family must get along and help each other. They understand that some kinds of trade are not fair to other countries. They see that they must work together to help all people.

The United Nations

Most countries in the world are members of the **United Nations (UN)**. Together, these countries can try to end problems in the world.

Two very important parts of the UN are the **General Assembly** and the **Security Council**. Each country sends representatives to the General Assembly. In the General Assembly, each country has one vote. The representatives in the General Assembly decide on the services of the UN for different countries in the world.

Five counties are always members of the Security Council. These countries are the United States, China, Russia, France, and England. These powerful countries are called the **Big Five**. Ten other countries can also be part of the Security Council. But they can be members of the Security Council only for two years.

In 1992, the United Nations sent soldiers, food, and other things to help people in Bosnia. Bosnia is in Eastern Europe.

The Security Council is the most powerful part of the United Nations. It tries to stop wars. It talks about fights between countries. The Security Council can also send special soldiers to stop these fights. These soldiers are from the member countries of the UN. They are soldiers for the UN army.

Sometimes, each member of the Security Council may have to decide if the UN should send soldiers to a certain country in the world. Each member of the Security Council can vote. But only a member of the Big Five has the power to veto. If one of the Big Five votes no, the Security Council cannot send soldiers to that part of the world.

The legislative branch of the state government of Illinois works in this building.

Chapter 9
The State Governments

The Constitution of the United States tells about the power of the federal government. It also tells about the power of the state governments.

There are 50 states. Each state has its own constitution and its own state government. Each state constitution tells how that state government works. The state governments are set up like the federal government. Each state government has three branches. These branches are the executive branch, the legislative branch, and the judicial branch. The branches of the state governments have to work together. They have checks and balances like the branches of the federal government.

How a state government works

In each state government, the **governor** is the leader of the executive branch. Most of the state governments also have a lieutenant governor. The lieutenant governor is a lot like the Vice President. The lieutenant governor helps the governor. The people in the state elect the governor and the lieutenant governor. Usually, the governor can pick the other workers for the executive branch.

The executive branch of the state government is like the executive branch of the federal government. The President makes plans for the federal government. The governor makes the plans for the state government. The governor thinks about the services of the state government. Then the governor makes the budget for the state government. The state budget tells about the money of the state government. It tells how the state government will spend its money for services.

The legislative branch has to vote about the state budget. If the representatives vote against the budget, the governor has to change it. The governor must work with the legislative branch on the budget. Then the legislative branch votes for the new state budget.

The governor can ask the representatives in the legislative branch to make laws. But the governor cannot make laws alone. Sometimes, the legislative branch makes these laws. Other times, it does not.

The legislative branch of each state government makes all the state laws. Some state laws tell how the state government will give services to the people in the state. Other state laws are about tax money for the services in the state. People in the state have to pay the state taxes. These taxes pay for the services in the state. Other state laws are about the crimes in the state. These laws tell how the state government will punish the lawbreakers. Everyone in the state has to obey the state criminal laws.

The legislative branch of the state government works like the legislative branch of the federal government. The legislative branch of most state governments has two parts. But in Nebraska, the legislative branch of the state government only has one part.

Governor Ann Richards speaks about the services of the state of Texas.

One part of the legislative branch is called the senate. The other part of the legislative branch has different names in different states. In most states, this part of the legislative branch is called the legislature. In some states it may be called the assembly, the house of representatives, or another name.

Each state has many areas or districts. Each district in the state has two senators in the state senate. The legislature is set up like the House of Representatives in the federal government. In the legislature, there are a different number of representatives from each district of the state. Some districts have many people. These districts can send many representatives to the legislature. Other areas in the state only have a few people. These areas send fewer representatives to the legislature.

The legislative branch of the state government passes some bills. Then it has to send these bills to the governor. The governor may sign these bills. Then these bills can become state laws. The governor may veto any bill from the state legislative branch. Then it cannot become a state law at that time. The legislative branch may vote about the bill again. Two out of every three representatives have to vote for the bill. Then it can become the law.

The state courts make up the judicial branch of the state government. These courts try to make sure that people obey the state laws. The state courts also try to make sure that the state and local governments obey the state constitution.

Judges in state courts listen to cases about state laws. The governor picks some people to be judges in some state courts. But the governor cannot tell the judges how to decide on a case. The governor cannot decide on the meaning of the state laws and state constitution.

Ways to make state laws

The legislative branch of the state government usually makes the state laws. But there are other ways to make state laws. Many state constitutions say how the people in the state can try to make state laws. These people do not have to be representatives in the state government.

People can try to make state laws in two ways. One way is called an **initiative**. An initiative is a special kind of bill. An initiative is also called a **proposition.**

Sometimes, some voters meet and decide that they want a certain kind of law. They write this initiative. The voters have to get many other voters to say that they want this initiative. When enough voters have signed this initiative, the state government must have an election. Then all the voters of the state can decide about this initiative. If more than half of the voters want this initiative, it becomes a state law. Then all people in the state have to obey this law.

Voters sign a paper to get a proposition on the ballot in the next election.

The other way to make a state law is called a **referendum**. Some state constitutions say that the voters in a state have to vote about certain kinds of bills. These bills are called referendums. Usually, referendums are about money. They say how the state government will pay for each service. Representatives cannot make referendums into laws by themselves.

Some representatives in the state legislature write a referendum. More than half of the representatives have to vote for the referendum. Then all the voters can vote about the referendum at the next election. More than half of the voters have to vote for the referendum. Then it becomes a state law.

Some state constitutions do not say that the people in their state can make laws in these ways. In these states, the legislative branch makes all of the laws. The voters cannot start initiatives. The representatives cannot start referendums.

The services of the state governments

Each state government gives many services to all of the people in its state. The budget of the state government tells how the state government will pay for each service. The legislative branch of a state government makes laws about each service.

For some services, the state government builds hospitals, schools, state office buildings, and roads. For other services, the state government runs the state police department, water department, and national guard. The state government also takes care of elections, licenses, poor people, and unemployment.

For some services, the state government has to make sure that workers know how to do their jobs. So state laws say that people have to pass a test about certain kinds of jobs. Then they get a special paper from the state government. This paper is called a **license**. These licenses say that these people are able to do a certain kind of work in the state. Teachers, doctors, lawyers, and other kinds of workers need licenses from the state government.

A state government also makes laws about other kinds of licenses. One kind of license is for marriage. When people get married, they have to get a marriage license from the state government.

Another kind of license is for drivers. Every driver must have a driver's license. State laws tell how people can get a driver's license from their state government. One of these state laws says that new drivers have to be a certain age. The new drivers cannot take the driving test before they are that age. Another state law tells about the driver's test.

In another service, a state government makes many different kinds of laws about companies. The state government has to know about all of the companies in the state. The state government makes sure that these companies obey all of the laws about companies. Some of these laws are about taxes on companies. Other state laws are about all workers in the state.

In another service, a state government tries to take care of the health of the people in the state. A state government runs certain hospitals in the state. It also makes laws about all hospitals in its state. These state laws tell what every hospital in the state has to do. These laws protect the people when they are in the hospital. The state government makes sure that all the hospitals in its state obey the laws about hospitals.

A state government makes laws about schools in its state, too. Some of these laws are about the age of the students. Other laws are about teachers and licenses. All of the public schools in the state have to obey the state laws about schools.

Each state government also makes laws about elections. Some of these laws tell when the state will have an election. Other state laws may be about voters in the state. For example, a state law may say that voters have to live in the state for six months. Then they can vote in the next election in the state.

Each state government has to make sure that the people in their state are safe. State governments may have many different kinds of police. Some state police take care of highways. Other state police help the local police departments. Other state police take care of state parks.

Each state government also has a national guard. The people in the national guard are like soldiers in the United States Army. But they work for the state government. The people in the national guard help other people when there is trouble in the state. For example, the national guard might help people in a bad snowstorm.

All state governments have services for the people in their state. One state government may not have the same services as another state. But in each state, the government has to have laws about each service in the state. The state laws about the same service may be different in different states. For example, in some states, a 16-year-old may get a driver's license. In other states, drivers must be at least 18 years old.

How state governments work together

Each state government gives many services to the people in the state. But the state governments may have to work together to give some services.

One state government may help another state government to make people obey state laws. For example, a person may have a driver's license from Maine. This person may drive in any state in the United States. This driver may drive in Ohio and break a law about driving in Ohio. The state police in Ohio may give a ticket to this driver. The driver from Maine may not pay this ticket. Then the state government of Maine may help the government of Ohio. The state government of Maine can make the driver from Maine pay for the ticket from Ohio.

State governments may also work together to deal with lawbreakers. For example, a person might break a law in Texas and move to Oklahoma. The police in Oklahoma may find the lawbreaker. The police must send the lawbreaker back to Texas. In Texas, the courts will have a trial for the lawbreaker.

Sometimes, more than one state government may have the same problem. So these state governments need to work together. Some of these problems may be about roads, water, or transportation. A group of representatives from each state government talk about the problem and the services of their state government. The representatives decide on how their state governments will take care of this problem. Then each state government makes laws. These laws tell how the services of each state government will take care of the problem.

For example, farmers and other people in Texas and Oklahoma wanted to use the water from the Red River.

A dam on the Red River makes sure that people in Oklahoma and Texas get enough water from the river.

The people in each state did not want the people in the other state to use too much of the water from this river. But each group needed to use some of this water. So the state governments of Texas and Oklahoma sent people to some meetings. These people from the state governments decided that dams on the Red River would protect the people in each state. These people also decided that people in each state could only take out a certain amount of water from the Red River. Then people in both states would have enough water. Both state governments passed the same law about the water in the Red River. One department in each state government makes sure that the people in its state obey the law.

How the federal and state governments work together

The federal government and the state governments give some of the same services. Each level of the government has to make laws about these services. But state governments cannot make laws against federal laws or the Constitution

Each state government has to take care of elections in its state. In this service, the state government makes laws about elections. It decides who may be a voter. For example, the Constitution says that voters must be at least 18 years old. A state law cannot say that a 16-year-old person may vote. A state law also cannot say that voters have to be 21 years old. But a state government can make a different kind of law about voters. A state law might say that voters have to live in the same place for three months. Then they can vote in the next election. This law is not against any federal law or the Constitution.

The federal government and the state governments work together on certain services. But the federal government and the state governments make their own laws about these services. The federal laws may say that the state governments have to give these services to the people.

The state government pays for part of these services. The federal government also gives money to the state governments for these services. The federal laws tell how the state governments must use this money. The state governments have to obey the federal laws about these services. Then the state governments can get the federal money for the services.

Sometimes, a state government may decide that it will not obey one federal law about a service. Then the federal government will not give any more money to that state government for that service. The state government can make laws about the service. But these laws cannot be against the federal laws.

For example, one federal service is to take care of the Social Security programs. These programs help poor people, sick people, and older people. The Social Security laws say that the federal government will pay money to the people in these programs. These laws say that all of the state governments must also pay their own money to poor people, sick people, and older people in their state. The state governments may make state laws about the amount of money for these programs. Then each of the state governments gives the federal money and the state money to the people in these programs.

New York City has its own local government.

Chapter 10
The Local Governments

There are many different areas in each state. Some of these may be large. Other areas may be small. But each area has its own government. The government for an area in the state is called a local government. It gives services to the people in its area.

Many people live in some areas of a state. These areas are called **urban** areas. Cities are in urban areas. The local governments in urban areas have to take care of services for many people.

Some towns and villages are near cities. These areas of the state are not part of the cities. These towns and villages are called **suburbs**. Many people live in suburbs and work in a city. Each town and village in the suburbs has its own local government.

Other areas of a state do not look like the urban areas or the suburbs. These areas are called rural areas. There are no cities, large towns, or large villages in rural areas. But rural areas have small towns and villages. Fewer people live in rural areas than in urban areas. Most farms are in rural areas. The local governments in rural areas have to take care of some services for the people in their areas.

Urban areas

Cities are urban areas. Each city must get a charter from its state government. The charter is like a constitution. Each charter tells how a city has to set up its local government.

A city government makes laws about the services for the people in the city. But a city government has to obey state laws and federal laws. The people in the city have to obey local, state, and federal laws.

Most city governments have three branches. These branches work together and give services. One branch is the executive branch. People in this branch make plans for the local government. Another branch is the legislative branch. It makes the laws for the local government. The other branch is the judicial branch. It runs the local courts. These courts deal with lawbreakers of local laws.

There are three different kinds of city governments. One kind of city government is called the Mayor and Council plan. Most large cities have this kind of city government. In this plan, the city government may have an executive branch, a legislative branch, and a judicial branch. Voters in the city elect the members of these branches of their city government.

KINDS OF CITY GOVERNMENT

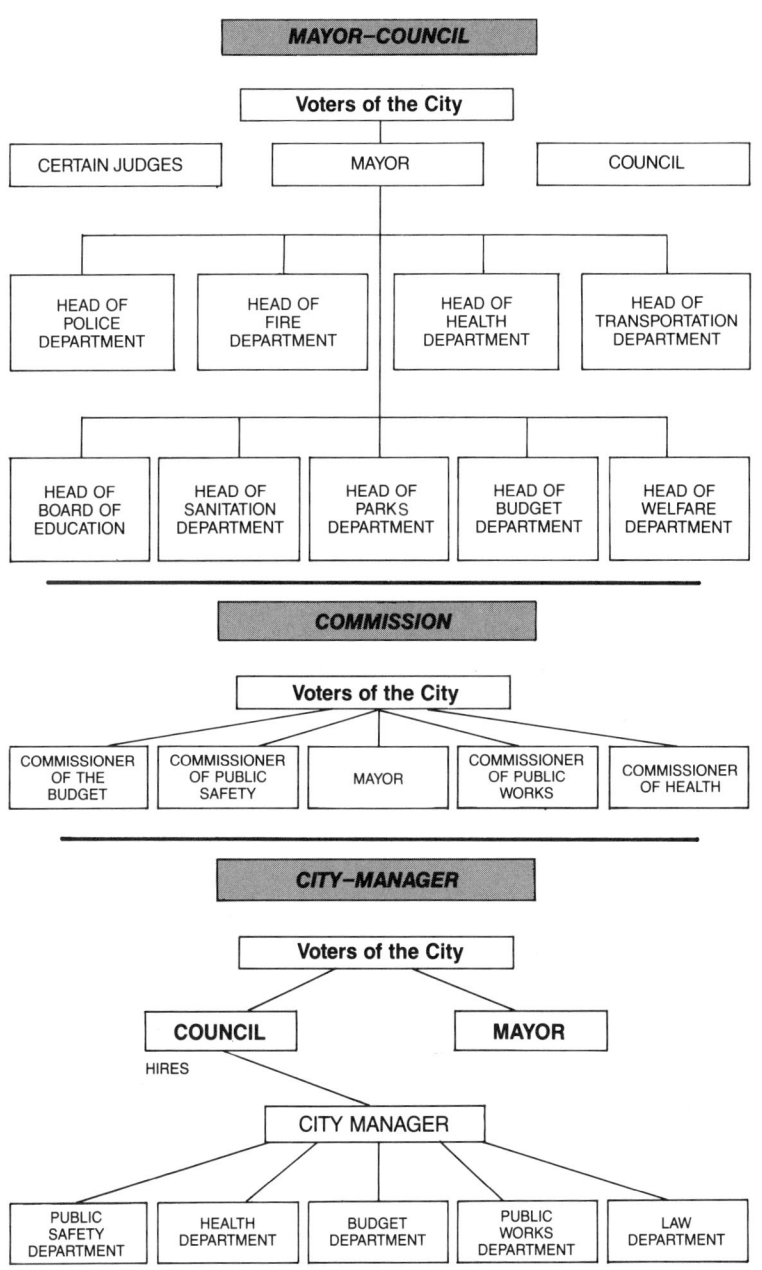

In the Mayor and Council plan, the leader of the executive branch is called the mayor. The mayor can pick a person to be the leader of each department in the city government. The mayor decides on the budget for the city government. The legislative branch is called the city council. The members of this council make the city laws. In some cities, the mayor has more power than the city council. In other cities, the city council has more power than the mayor. The judicial branch decides if people have broken the local laws.

Another kind of city government is called the Commission plan. In this plan, the voters elect a small group of commissioners. The commissioners are both the legislative branch and the executive branch of the city

The town hall of North Hempstead, New York.

government. Together, the commissioners make the laws for the city government. Each commissioner is also the leader of one of the city departments. Together, the commissioners can pick other people to take care of other departments in the city.

The other kind of city government is called the Council and Manager plan. In this plan, the legislative branch is called the city council. Voters must elect the members of the city council. The city council makes the laws for the city. The members of the city council hire a city manager. The city manager is the leader of the executive branch of the city government. The city manager picks people to take care of all the city departments.

All towns and villages also have their own local governments. But they do not have charters. The state government decides on the kind of government for each town or village in the state. Many of these local governments are like city governments. They might have three branches in their government. Other governments of towns and villages might have only one branch.

County governments

Each state government has made special areas out of all the land in its state. In each area, there may be cities, towns, and villages. In most states, these areas are called counties. In Louisiana, they are called parishes. In Alaska, they are called boroughs. There is a government for each county, parish, or borough.

Each county government is a part of its state government. Each county government helps the state government to carry out the state laws. The state government tells each county government what it has to do. Then the county government takes care of certain services for the state government.

County governments are not like other kinds of local governments. They do not have three branches. In most counties, the county government is called the county board. Voters have to elect people to be the members of the county board. Most county boards cannot make laws. In rural areas, county governments are the strongest local governments.

Other members of a county government are the sheriff, the county clerk, and the county attorney. Voters also elect these representatives in their county governments. The sheriff is the leader of the police department in the county government. The sheriff has to make sure that all people in the county obey all state laws. The county clerk keeps certain important papers for the people in the county. Some of these papers are about marriages, births, deaths, and land.

The county attorney is the lawyer for the state. This person takes care of the cases in the county court. These cases are about state laws and local laws. The county attorney may also be called the district attorney.

The services of the local governments

A local government takes care of many services for the people in its area. In urban areas, the local governments may be large. A lot of people work for these local governments. These governments have a lot of services for the people in their area. In rural areas, most local governments are small. Only a few people work for these local governments. These governments give fewer services to the people in their area.

A local government may have many different departments. Each department takes care of a different service. Some of these departments are the board of education, the police department, the fire department, the sanitation department, the water department, and the transportation department.

Local governments may say that the people in their area have to pay local taxes. A local government may also get money from its state government and the federal government. All of this money pays for the services of the local government.

A fire department in a rural area.

In each state, the local governments run the schools in their area. The local government hires the teachers and other workers in these schools. Local governments also make the rules about the teachers and the students in these schools. The local governments also make the budget for these schools.

Local governments also run the police department in their area. A police department tries to keep people safe. It makes sure that people do not break local and state laws. Each police department also tries to find lawbreakers.

In urban areas, the fire department is usually part of the local government. In rural areas, the local government usually does not pay for a local fire department. But some people in the area become the firefighters for the area. The local government does not pay these firefighters for their work.

Another service of the local governments is the sanitation department. This department takes care of the garbage. In most urban areas, trucks from this department take the garbage from houses and other buildings. In some rural areas, people have to bring their garbage to a dump. The sanitation department takes care of the dump. Another service of the local government is a water department. This department makes sure that people have enough clean water in their buildings.

Local governments have to think about the need for transportation in their area. A local government takes care of the streets, roads and highways in its area. It builds roads and fixes them. In cities, the department of transportation usually runs the buses and subways.

The local governments have to make sure that the buildings in their area are safe. They can make laws about buildings. The local government makes sure that people obey these laws.

Local governments may also give other services to the people. A local government may own hospitals. It may take care of parks and swimming pools.

Local governments may make laws about each of their services. Sometimes, people break the local laws. The local governments have courts. These courts decide if a person has broken a local law. Then the local government punishes a lawbreaker. For example, a local law says that people cannot park cars in front of a firehouse. Local police can put tickets on these cars. The owners of these cars may have to pay for these tickets in a local court.

How local governments work with the federal and state governments

The local governments get some of their power from the state government. Local laws can never go against state laws or federal laws. The state government says that local governments can make laws by themselves. Then local governments can make people obey these local laws.

The federal government gives money to local governments for school buses in their area.

Some state laws say that the local governments must give certain services to the people in their area. Other state laws say that the local governments do not have to

87

give certain services to the people. For example, all local governments must have schools for the children in their area. But all local governments do not have to pay people to be firefighters in their area.

Local governments may give the same kinds of services as the state and federal governments. The local government has to obey the state and federal laws about each of these services. Most of the time, local governments obey the federal and state laws. Then they get money from the state and federal governments.

Other times, a local government does not obey a part of a state law or a federal law about a service. Then the state or federal government does not give money for that service to the local government. The state or federal government gives money to the local government only if the local government decides to obey their laws about that service.

For example, the local government runs the schools in its area. But it also gets money from the state government and the federal government for this service. Sometimes, a local government does not obey a state law about schools. Then the state government does not have to give all the money for the schools to the local government. At other times, the local government does not obey a federal law about schools. So the federal government does not have to give all the money for the schools to the local government.

The three levels of American government have many services for the people in the United States. All of the levels of government work together to protect people and help people live together peacefully. Americans elect the members of their government. So Americans can change their representatives. When the needs of the people change, the government of the United States can change. It can change the services for the people. In this way, the American government is a government by the people and for the people.

GLOSSARY

amendment A new part of the Constitution. An amendment adds a new idea or changes an old idea about how the government works or about people's rights.

Big Five A group of five countries in the United Nations. These countries are the most powerful on the Security Council. (*See also* Security Council, United Nations.)

bill A written plan for a law. A bill may change many times before it becomes a law.

Bill of Rights The first ten amendments to the Constitution. They tell about the rights of all Americans.

budget A special plan for the money of the government. The budget tells how much money the government has and how it will spend this money.

Cabinet A special group of people in the executive branch. Each member of the Cabinet is the head of a department in the executive branch. (*See also* Secretary.)

campaign The effort made to get people to vote for someone in an election. A part of a campaign can be speeches, ads and letters to people.

campaign contribution A gift of money made to help another person win an election.

checks and balances The ways one branch of government makes sure that another branch of government does not have too much power. Checks and balances are part of the Constitution.

communist government A government that owns most of the companies in the country. China and Cuba have communist governments.

Communist Party The political party in a country with a communist government.

Congress The legislative branch of the federal government. Congress makes the federal laws. It is made up of the Senate and the House of Representatives.

Congressional district Special areas in each state. Each Congressional district is based on the number of people in the area. There are 435 Congressional districts in the United States.

Constitution A plan for setting up the government. The Constitution of the United States was signed in 1789. American government today is still based on the Constitution. (*See also* amendment.)

democracy A kind of government. In a democracy, people have many rights. They can choose the people that they want to run their government. (*See also* representative.)

dictator The leader in a country without a democratic government.

elect To choose representatives in a democracy. The person with the most votes is elected.

executive branch One of the three branches of government. The executive branch makes plans for the government and carries out the laws.

federal government The government of all of the United States.

General Assembly A part of the United Nations. Every member has representatives in the General Assembly. (*See also* Security Council, United Nations.)

governor The leader of the executive branch of a state government.

House of Representatives One of the two parts of the Congress of the United States. It has 435 Representatives.

initiative A bill started by people in a state. An initiative may also be called a proposition.

judicial branch One of the three branches of government. The judicial branch is made up of the courts.

legislative branch One of the three branches of government. The legislative branch writes the laws of the government.

license A special paper that a government gives to certain people, for example, a doctor's license or a driver's license.

lobby To talk to government representatives in order to ask them to vote in a certain way. (*See also* lobbyist.)

lobbyist A person paid to lobby. (*See also* lobby.)

local government The government of a county, city, or town.

proposition Another name for an initative. (*See also* initiative.)

referendum A special kind of bill in a state legislature. The people in the state must vote for the bill before it can become a law.

representative A member of the government in a democracy. The people vote for representatives in a democracy.

rights The freedoms people have under their government. Usually, these freedoms are written down.

Secretary The title of each member of the Cabinet, for example the Secretary of Defense or Secretary of State. (*See also* Cabinet.)

Security Council The most powerful part of the United Nations. (*See also* Big Five, United Nations.)

Senate One of the two parts of the Congress of the United States. It has 100 members.

Soviet Union The old name of the country now called Russia. The name was changed in 1991, when the government of the Soviet Union fell apart.

state government The government of each of the 50 states in the United States.

suburb An area outside of a city.

Supreme Court The highest court in the judicial branch of the federal government. The Supreme Court decides if laws agree with the Constitution.

Third World The poor countries of Asia, Africa, and parts of Latin America.

treaty A written agreement between countries.

United Nations (UN) A group of countries in the world. The United Nations tries to keep peace in the world. (*See also* General Assembly, Security Council.)

urban area An area with a lot of people. Urban areas may be cities or large towns.

veto A vote against a bill by an executive. A President or a governor has the power to veto a bill.